Fact Finders®

Biographies

Eva Perón

First Lady of the People

by Kremena Spengler

Consultant:
Richard J. Walter, PhD
Professor of History
Washington University in St. Louis
St. Louis, Missouri

Capstone
press®

Mankato, Minnesota

Fact Finders is published by Capstone Press,
151 Good Counsel Drive, P.O. Box 669, Mankato, Minnesota 56002.
www.capstonepress.com

Library of Congress Cataloging-in-Publication Data
Spengler, Kremena.
    Eva Perón : first lady of the people / by Kremena Spengler.
    p. cm.—(Fact Finders. Biographies. Great Hispanics)
    Includes bibliographical references and index.
    ISBN-13: 978-0-7368-6415-2 (hardcover)
    ISBN-10: 0-7368-6415-6 (hardcover)
    1. Perón, Eva, 1919–1952—Juvenile literature. 2. Argentina—History—1943–1955—Juvenile literature. 3. Women politicians—Argentina—Biography—Juvenile literature.
4. Presidents' spouses—Argentina—Biography—Juvenile literature. I. Title. II. Series.
F2849.P37S64 2007
982'.06092—dc22   2005037727

Summary: An introduction to the life of Eva Perón, the first lady of Argentina from 1946 to 1952, who fought for workers' rights and political power for women.

Editorial Credits
John Bliss and Jennifer Murtoff (Navta Associates), editors; Juliette Peters, set designer;
    Lisa Zucker, book designer; Wanda Winch, photo researcher/photo editor

Photo Credits
AP/Wide World Photos/Archivo Clarin, 25; Corbis/Bettmann, cover, 8, 12, 19, 20; Corbis/Hulton-Deutsch Collection, 7, 9; Getty Images Inc./AFP, 1, 5, 13, 16, 21, 24, 27; Getty Images Inc./Hulton Archive, 17; Getty Images Inc./Keystone, 11; Getty Images Inc./Time Life Pictures/Thomas D. McAvoy, 15, 26; Getty Images Inc./Time Life Pictures/Time Magazine, Copyright Time Inc./Time Life Pictures, 23

1 2 3 4 5 6 11 10 09 08 07 06

Table of Contents

Chapter 1

Lady of Hope

Eva Perón's office was packed with men, women, and children. Many of them were poor and hopeless. They had heard that the president's wife could help them.

Suddenly, a whisper went around the room. "Here she comes!" Perón, lovingly called Evita, walked briskly into the room. Lights flashed, shining on her blonde hair. To the crowd, she looked like an angel.

Perón's first visitor on this day in 1949 was a woman who lived in one room with her eight children. Perón quickly filled out a sheet of paper. The woman had asked for a house. Perón gave her a house, as well as a large bed and clothing.

Perón sat at her desk for hours, helping poor people in Argentina.

The stream of visitors continued. Argentina's most powerful woman had once been poor. She made sure no one was turned away. Perón would give the people all she could.

Chapter 2

Perón's Childhood

On May 7, 1919, a girl was born in the small, dusty village of Los Toldos, Argentina. The baby, María Eva, was the youngest of five children.

The children's father, Juan Duarte, was a local landowner. He was not married to their mother, Juana Ibarguren. He had another family in a nearby town.

Juan Duarte left when Perón was less than a year old. Ibarguren and the children stayed in Los Toldos. Without Duarte's support, the family had to move into a one-room house. To feed her children, Ibarguren sewed clothes for others. The family had very little money.

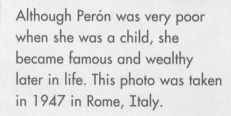

Although Perón was very poor
when she was a child, she
became famous and wealthy
later in life. This photo was taken
in 1947 in Rome, Italy.

As a child, Perón did not have many friends. Some children would not play with her because her parents were not married. Perón played with her sisters and brother. She would wear homemade costumes and pretend to be someone else.

In school, Perón loved poetry and movies. She read movie magazines and collected pictures of movie stars.

Canadian-born actress Norma Shearer was a role model for Perón. ▼

A Dream

Perón dreamed of being an actress. To make her dream come true, she decided to go to Buenos Aires. Argentina's capital was a large city, with theaters, radio stations, and movie companies. Her mother was not happy with Perón's decision. But she did not stop her daughter.

When she was 15, Perón decided to go to Buenos Aires, the capital of Argentina, to become an actress. ⬇

9

Chapter 3

An Actress Meets a Workers' Hero

At age 15, Perón arrived in Buenos Aires. She found a cheap place to live and started to look for acting parts.

Perón's first parts were in plays. The parts were small and hard to get. Perón had little money and often went hungry.

Perón did not give up. At age 18, she landed her first movie role. She also got jobs acting in radio programs. At that time, people listened to shows on the radio instead of watching television. On the radio, Perón starred in programs about famous women in history.

In Buenos Aires, Perón, third from left, performed in radio programs. This photo was taken in 1944.

QUOTE

"Very early in life I left my home and my hometown and since then I've always lived free. I've wanted to be on my own, and I have been on my own."

—Eva Perón

Juan Perón

In 1944, when Eva Perón was 24, she started dating a member of the military government, Colonel Juan Perón. He helped workers' groups as part of his job with the government. Unlike other leaders, he raised wages and gave workers sick leave and other rights. His actions made him popular with the workers. But there were many people in government who did not like what he was doing.

▲ As a teenager, Juan Perón attended a military academy.

F A C T !

Eva Perón met Juan Perón at a festival to raise money for people hurt by an earthquake.

▲ Eva Perón and Juan Perón often made public appearances together.

Eva Perón often went with Juan Perón to political events. This upset some leaders, who thought that women should not be involved in politics.

Government officials who didn't like Juan Perón's policies had him arrested and forced him to resign. But the workers demanded his freedom. They were later called *descamisados,* ("shirtless ones"). Over 200,000 workers marched into the streets of Buenos Aires.

Chapter 4

First Lady

The government could not ignore the people's protests for Juan Perón's release. Four days after his arrest, Juan Perón was set free.

Juan Perón knew he had the support of the workers. He began a **campaign** to become president of Argentina.

On October 22, 1945, Juan Perón and Eva Perón were married. As a wife, Eva Perón was expected to stay at home. Instead, she joined her husband's campaign. Eva Perón handed out buttons and greeted people. She campaigned hard for her husband. Soon, she became as well known as Juan Perón himself.

Eva Perón supported her husband as he campaigned for president.

Helping the People

With his wife's help, Juan Perón won the 1946 election. At age 27, Eva Perón became Argentina's first lady. Unlike any first lady before her, Eva Perón set out to help the workers. She helped solve problems between bosses and workers. She helped the workers get pay raises and better working conditions. She helped them get better health care and money for retirement. Perón spoke to large crowds and built up support for her husband.

Eva Perón and her husband (center) read the paper announcing that he won the 1946 ▼ presidential election.

16

Perón helped women gain the right to vote. Here she speaks to a large crowd of women in August of 1951.

Perón also wanted to help women in Argentina. She helped pass a law that gave women the right to vote. In 1949, she formed the new Peronist Women's Party. The **party** spread Juan Perón's ideas among women. In 1951, her party would help reelect her husband. Its members would become the first women ever to serve in Argentina's Congress.

Chapter 5

Two Views of Perón

When Perón became first lady, people started to ask for things they needed. Perón began to collect things, such as shoes, pots, and flour, for the poor. She stored them in an empty garage at her home. At night, as her husband slept, Perón made packages for the poor.

Building a Foundation

To help meet people's needs, Perón created more projects. To pay for them, she started the María Eva Duarte de Perón **Foundation** in 1948. The foundation's money came from the government, workers' groups, and employers.

MUNICIPALIDAD
DE LA
CIUDAD INFANTIL

⬆ Perón founded the Children's City in Buenos Aires, a place where children with family problems could live.

FACT!

Perón started soccer games for children. The games gave doctors a chance to give the children checkups.

The foundation used the money to build thousands of schools, hospitals, and homes for children and poor people. The schools and hospitals had the best equipment. The homes had fine furnishings. Perón chose everything herself.

▲ Perón worked hard for the *descamisados*, and they loved her.

Controversy

The *descamisados* loved Perón. They called her Evita, or "little Eva." But wealthy Argentines disliked her. They made fun of her poor background. They thought she spent too much money on clothes and jewels for herself. Perón accepted expensive gifts from people who wanted to gain her good will. She put members of her own family in important jobs and helped them become rich. This made some people angry.

QUOTE

"I am Eva Perón, the wife of the president, whose work is simple and agreeable. . . and I am also Evita, the wife of the leader of a people who have deposited in him all their faith, hope, and love."
—Eva Perón

Perón spent a lot of money on fancy clothing and jewelry. Some citizens thought she was too extravagant.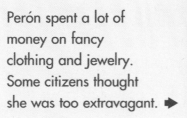

People who did not like Perón were afraid of speaking up. Sometimes people who disagreed with the government lost their jobs or went to jail.

Chapter 6

Final Honors

Perón became well known outside Argentina. She toured Europe and met the Pope. The U.S. magazine *Time* put her picture on the cover.

In Argentina, Perón's picture was everywhere. Newspapers often printed articles about her with large photos. Schools, hospitals, streets, and even a newly discovered star were named after her. People wrote songs about her. The workers even wanted her to run for vice president.

What the people did not know was that Perón's health was failing. **Cancer** had spread in her body. The weaker she grew, the harder she worked.

TIME

THE WEEKLY NEWSMAGAZINE

EVA PERÓN
Between two worlds, an Argentine rainbow.

Boris Chaliapin

⬆ Perón was featured on the July 14, 1947,
cover of *Time* magazine.

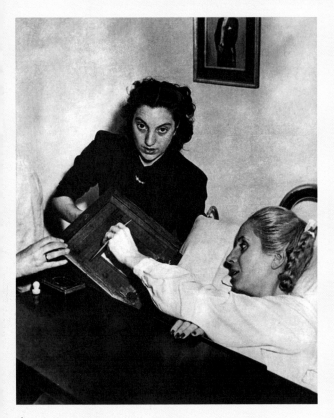

On November 11, 1951, a very sick Perón voted from her hospital bed. It was the first and last time she voted.

Saying Good-Bye

Perón died on July 26, 1952. She was 33 years old. Millions of people came to say good-bye to her. They lined up for more than 15 hours in the rain to see her. Women fainted with grief. Flowers were piled 20 feet (6 meters) high up the wall of the building where her body lay.

For days after Perón died, no business was carried out in Argentina. Trains stopped. Stores closed. Guests in fine hotels had to make their own beds.

▲ Thousands of people came to watch Perón's funeral procession in Buenos Aires.

QUOTE

"Wherever Perón may be and wherever my *descamisados* may be, there, too, my heart will always be, to love them with all the strength left of my life, and all the fanaticism burning in my soul."

—Eva Perón

Because of her strong public presence, Perón had become a big part of people's lives. They could not imagine the country without her.

Lasting Legacy

Without his wife's support, Juan Perón's rule was ended by the military. Later governments tried to make people forget Eva Perón. They destroyed her projects.

But the *descamisados* would never forget her. Perón helped them gain rights and power for the first time in Argentina's history. For them, Eva Perón had become a saint.

◄ Perón was a saint to her beloved *descamisados*.

Fast Facts

Full name: María Eva Duarte de Perón

Birth: May 7, 1919

Death: July 26, 1952

Parents: Juan Duarte and Juana Ibarguren

Siblings: Elisa, Blanca, Erminda, Juan

Hometown: Los Toldos, Argentina; later Buenos Aires

Husband: Juan Domingo Perón, president of Argentina

Achievements:

First lady of Argentina, 1946–1952

Founded the María Eva Duarte de Perón Foundation

Started the Peronist Women's Party

Wrote a book about her life, *La razón de mi vida (The Reason for My Life)*

Time Line

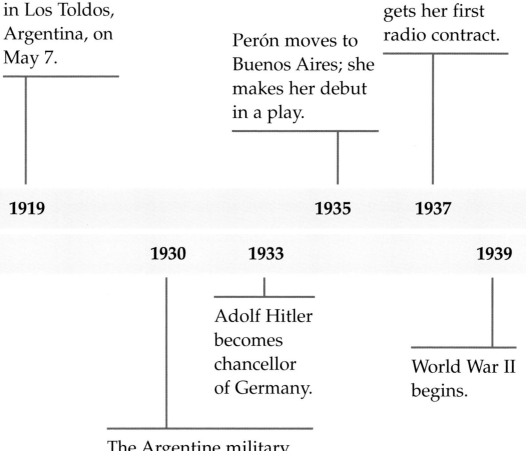

Life Events of Eva Perón

María Eva Duarte is born in Los Toldos, Argentina, on May 7.

Perón moves to Buenos Aires; she makes her debut in a play.

Perón debuts in a movie; she gets her first radio contract.

1919   **1935**   **1937**

1930   **1933**   **1939**

Events in World History

Adolf Hitler becomes chancellor of Germany.

World War II begins.

The Argentine military forces the president out of office and takes control of the government.